The Irish Vanguard Of Rhode Island

Thomas Hamilton Murray

In the interest of creating a more extensive selection of rare historical book reprints, we have chosen to reproduce this title even though it may possibly have occasional imperfections such as missing and blurred pages, missing text, poor pictures, markings, dark backgrounds and other reproduction issues beyond our control. Because this work is culturally important, we have made it available as a part of our commitment to protecting, preserving and promoting the world's literature. Thank you for your understanding.

THE
IRISH VANGUARD
OF
RHODE ISLAND.

BY THOMAS HAMILTON MURRAY

Author of Papers on: Five Colonial Rhode Islanders; Early Irish Schoolmasters
in Rhode Island; Charles MacCarthy, a Founder of East Greenwich, R. I.;
The Dorrance Purchase — A Leaf from Rhode Island History; The
Irish Chapter in the History of Brown University; Thomas
Casey of Ireland and Rhode Island; Reminiscences of Life
Along Narragansett's Shores; Rambles in Rhode
Island's South County; Gen. John Sullivan
and the Battle of Rhode Island; Etc.

BOSTON, MASS.
Reprinted from Vol. IV, Journal of the American-Irish Historical Society
1904

SOME VOICES FROM YE OLDEN TIME.

BY THOMAS HAMILTON MURRAY, BOSTON, MASS.

Alexander Gilligan was a resident of Marblehead, Mass., in 1674.

Many Irish participated in the settlement of Salem, N. Y., in 1765. (*The Salem Book.*)

Samuel and Robert Elder, brothers, came from Ireland about 1730 and settled in Falmouth, Me.

In 1746 a marriage license was issued, Spottsylvania, Va., to Patrick Connelly and Ann French.

Dennis Lochlin, of Putney, Vt., was a representative to the General Assembly of that state in 1777.

Lucy Todd O'Brien married, in 1698, John Baylor of Gloucester county, Va. (*Virginia Historical Magazine.*)

The records of Braintree, Mass., note the birth "6th mo. 18. 1669" of Samuel Daly, a son of John and Elizabeth Daly.

Timothy Hierlehey was captain of the seventh company of the First Regiment of the Colony of Connecticut, 1758.

Rev. James Tate, a Presbyterian minister from Ireland, organized Tate's Academy, in Wilmington, N. C., about 1760.

At a great fire in Boston, Mass., 1787, among those whose premises were burned were Dennis Welch and Andrew Kalley.

Capt. Wm. McGinnis, with 89 men of Schenectady, N. Y., was at the battle near Fort George, Sept. 8, 1755, and was killed there.

About 1762–'65, Rev. Ezra Stiles, of Newport, R. I., acknowledges having received from Capt. Jno. Nichols a firkin of "Irish butter."

James Warren settled at South Berwick, Me., as early as 1656. He was a native of Scotland; his wife, Margaret, a native of Ireland.

On May 14, 1663, Miles More and Michael Rice of New London were accepted as freemen by the General Assembly of Connecticut.

Among the men serving under Capt. John Gilman, New Hampshire, in 1710, were Daniel Lary, Thomas Lary and Jeremiah Connor.

Major William Waters, son of Capt. Edward and Grace (O'Neil) Waters, patented land in Maryland as early as 1663. He left six sons.

We learn in Frothingham's *Charlestown, Mass.*, that in 1640 "there came over great store of provisions both out of England and Ireland."

Edwin Larkin was located at Newport, R. I., as early as 1655. His name appears in the "Roule of y*e* Freemen of y*e* colonie of everie Towne."

Several years previous to 1686, "persons from Ireland, picked up at sea and brought hither, have £17 given them." (Felt's *Annals of Salem, Mass.*)

As early as 1636, Edward Brick, or Breck, and his son Robert, "of Galway in Ireland," are heard from in Dorchester, now a part of Boston, Mass.

In 1659 "John Morrell an Irishman and Lysbell Morrell an Irishwoman were married 31st August by John Endecott," Governor. (*Boston, Mass., Records.*)

John Casey, James Brannon, John Bryan and James Moore were among the field officers appointed by the Provincial Congress of North Carolina, in 1776.

Cornelius Conner witnessed a deed (conveyance of real estate), in 1665, by John Clough of Salisbury, Mass. (*The Essex Antiquarian*, Salem, Mass., Jan., 1902.)

Among the soldiers at Fort William and Mary, N. H., in 1708, were John Foy, Jeremiah Libby, John Neal, Samuel Neal, John Mead and Timothy Blake.

John Donaldson, an Irishman, commanded, during the Revolution, an armed brig of 10 guns and carrying 45 men. He was at one time a resident of Salem, Mass.

Stephen Decatur, Sr., married "a young lady named Pine, the

daughter of an Irish gentleman." Stephen Decatur, the distinguished naval officer, was their son.

Samuel Neale, Quaker, was born in Dublin, Ireland, 1729. He came to this country, and in 1772 preached at Newport, R. I. He died in Cork, Ireland, 1792.

John Moore, "formerly of Dublin," is mentioned in Charlestown, Mass., about 1680. He was a shipwright. (Wyman's *Genealogies and Estates of Charlestown.*)

The Massachusetts records show that in 1661 "John Reylean an Irishman & Margaret Brene an Irishwoman were married 15th March by John Endecott Governor."

From the files of York County, Me., we learn that Thomas Crowley, and his wife Joanna, had a daughter Arpira Sayward who had a son Samuel, born about 1668.

Roger Kelley was representative from the Isles of Shoals at the first General Court of Massachusetts under the new charter, 1692. (Farmer's *Genealogical Register.*)

Joseph McDowell and his wife, Margaret O'Neal, came from Ireland to Winchester, Va., about 1743. Two of their sons became distinguished in the Revolution.

Hon. Charles Jackson, Governor of Rhode Island, 1845-'46, was a descendant of Stephen Jackson, a native of Kilkenny, Ireland, who came to this country about 1724.

Col. James Moore, who commanded the First Regiment of North Carolina Continentals in the Revolution, was of the Irish Moores who had settled in that part of the country.

In Felt's *Annals of Salem, Mass.,* is found mention, 1789, of "John Brenon from Dublin," who "performs on the slackwire, balances and gives specimens of legerdemain."

Charles MacCarthy was one of the founders of the town of East Greenwich, R. I., 1677. He had previously resided in St. Kitts. He had a brother who went from Ireland to Spain.

The oldest Irish organization in this country is the Charitable Irish Society, Boston, Mass. It was founded in 1737, and is still enjoying a prosperous existence. Gen. Henry Knox was a member.

Thomas McDonoghue was a resident of Charlestown, Mass., in

1798. John Russell married Mary Malonie in 1772. Russell is heard of as early as 1769. (Wyman's *Charlestown*.)

Kennedy O'Brien was one of the early residents of Augusta, Ga. He was a merchant. A deposition made by him in 1741 is mentioned. (*Collections of the Georgia Historical Society*.)

According to Felt's *Annals of Salem, Mass.*, Butler Fogarty was a school teacher there in 1792. He gave up his school to become clerk of the Essex bank, but in 1794 went back to teaching.

St. Patrick's Lodge of Masons was instituted at Johnstown, N. Y., in 1766. Another lodge bearing the same name was located at Portsmouth, N. H., and was chartered March 17, 1780.

Edward Jones, of Wilmington, N. C., a native of Ireland, was elected to the North Carolina House of Commons in 1788 and served until 1791, when he became Solicitor-General of the state.

Edward Rigg, an Irishman, died in New York city, 1786. He was for many years a school teacher there. Edward Fogarty, another school teacher, died in New York city about the same time.

Hon. Edward Kavanagh became governor of the state of Maine on the resignation of Governor Fairfield, 1843. Governor Kavanagh's father was a native of New Ross, County Wexford, Ireland.

Savage's *Genealogical Dictionary* of New England states that in 1654 Edward Welch, "an Irish youth," was sent over, by the ruling power in England, in the ship *Goodfellow*, "to be sold here."

John Campbell, who was twice speaker of the North Carolina House of Assembly, was reared in Coleraine, Ireland. He was "a wise and thrifty man." (Moore's *History of North Carolina*.)

Among the members of Capt. Fullwood's Company of volunteers, South Carolina, 1775, were William Martin, William McCoy, John Laferty, Patrick Fagan, Robert Reilly and Cornelius Donavan.

It is stated that in 1720 the Irish of Lancaster County, Pennsylvania, were excused from rents "in consideration of their being a frontier people forming a kind of cordon of defence if needful."

Allan Mullins, surgeon, son of Dr. Alexander Mullins of Galway, Ireland, was married to Abigail, daughter of John Butler, of New London, Conn., April 8, 1725. (*New London Marriage Records*.)

In Pearson's *Genealogies*, relating to the "Ancient County of

Albany, N. Y.," is mentioned Pieter Macarty of Half Moon who, in 1736, married Greefje Rhee. His second wife (1742) was Anna Abt.

Nicholas Rowe is mentioned at Portsmouth, N. H., in 1640, and Matthew Rowe at New Haven, Conn., in 1650. The latter had three sons,—John, Joseph and Stephen. (Farmer's *Genealogical Register*.)

Arthur Dobbs, governor of North Carolina, took the oath at Newbern in 1754. "He was an Irishman and had been a member of the parliament of that country." (Moore's *History of North Carolina*.)

Daniel Neil was captain-lieutenant of Frelinghuysen's Eastern Company of Artillery (New Jersey state troops), and subsequently commanded the same. He was killed at the battle of Princeton, 1777.

In 1674 there were nine Catholic religious confraternities in St. Augustine, Florida, one of them being under the patronage of St. Patrick. (John Gilmary Shea in *The Catholic Church in Colonial Days*.)

The Fellowship Club was organized at Newport, R. I., in Dec., 1752. The first meeting was held at the Black Horse Inn. John Murphy was admitted to membership in 1803, and William Callahan in 1817.

In Wyman's *Genealogies and Estates of Charlestown, Mass.*, is mentioned Edward Larkin, a wheel-maker. He was admitted an inhabitant in 1638. His wife was Joanna. A son was named John Larkin.

A return of the men enlisted by Lieut. Henry Piercy of the Second Pennsylvania Regiment, 1778, mentions Patrick McQuire, a native of Ireland, 42 years of age, and says that he "has the brogue on his tongue."

The provincial congress of North Carolina, 1776, appointed James Hogan paymaster of the Third Regiment and also of the three companies of Light Horse. (Wheeler's *Historical Sketches of North Carolina*.)

Thomas Burke was chosen governor of North Carolina in 1781. He was an Irishman by birth and had been educated for a physician. He came to America long prior to the Revolution and first settled at Norfolk, Va.

We learn from the published records of Providence, R. I., that, in 1682, Cornelius Higgins bought of Andrew Harris, of Pawtucket, R. I., 98 1-4 acres in Scituate, in the "precincts of y* said Town* of Providence."

John Keeney and Thomas Roach of New London, Conn., were nominated for freemen at the General Court, opened in Connecticut on Oct. 14, 1669. Timothy Forde was nominated for freeman on May 14, 1668.

John, Daniel and Nancy O'Brien were residents of New London, Conn., in 1795. John Callahan and Henry McCabe were there in 1796. Patrick Mann and John Sweeney were residents of Hartford, Conn., in 1799.

It is said of Arthur Dobbs, an Irish governor of North Carolina (1754), that he brought over a few pieces of artillery, one thousand muskets "and a plentiful supply of his poor relations." (Moore's *North Carolina*.)

James Coleman, Maurice Murphey, Jr., Matthew Murphey, John Kenneday, and Francis Kenneday were among the organizers of a military company on the northeast side of the Pee Dee river, South Carolina, in 1775.

On Aug. 16, 1688, at Northfield, Mass., three men, two women and a girl were killed by the Indians. One of the victims was John Clary, father of the John Clary who was killed at Brookfield, Mass., in 1709. (*Temple.*)

John Neil, from Ireland, was in Scituate, Mass., as early as 1730. He established a pottery thereabouts. Edward Humphries, from Ireland, was a resident of Scituate as far back as 1740. (Deane's *History of Scituate*.)

Thomas Donohoe was major of the Sixth Regiment, North Carolina Foot, organized at Hillsborough, 1776. He became a member of the Society of the Cincinnati at the latter's inception at Newburg, on the Hudson, 1783.

The records of the Church of Christ, Bristol, R. I., note the baptism, in 1712, of Bridget, daughter of James and Bridget Cary. In 1747, is noted the baptism of Michael and Bridget Phillips, children of Michael and Bridget.

Among the old New York families may be mentioned the Van

Bergens of Catskill and Coxsackie. Elizabeth Van Bergen, born in 1781, married Richard McCarty. One of her children married a daughter of John McCarty.

John Casey of Muddy River (now Brookline, Mass.) was a participant in King Philip's war, 1675–'76. He took part in the attack on the Indian fort in "the Great Swamp," Rhode Island, and was wounded in that engagement.

A prominent regiment in the American Revolution was the First Pennsylvania line. The regimental rolls show over 200 typical Irish surnames, some of them being several times repeated, borne by different members of the command.

The 30th of 11th mo., 1642. "John Smith, Gent., his assessment of ————, unto the last county rate, is remitted unto him, upon consideration of the great losses that have of late befallen him in Ireland." (*Boston Town Records.*)

In 1767–'68, the British warship *Cygnet* wintered at New London, Conn. The purser of the ship bore the name John Sullivan. Becoming enamored of civil life as well as of Elizabeth Chapman, he married and settled in New London.

James Stacpole, born in 1652, was probably a son of Philip, of Limerick, Ireland. James was living in Dover, N. H. (Rollinsford), in 1680. He died in 1736. The name is also spelled Stackpole. (Stackpole's *History of Durham, Me.*)

Alfred Moore, Sr., of North Carolina, was a son of Judge Maurice Moore and nephew of Col. James Moore who commanded the First Regiment, North Carolina Continentals, during the Revolution. Alfred was a captain in the regiment.

David Flanagan is buried at Bedford, Westchester County, N. Y. He was born in Dublin, Ireland, in 1759. During the Revolution he was clerk on board a vessel of the American navy. He subsequently became a bookseller, and died in 1805.

At a great Boston fire, 1760, Michael Carroll and Capt. Killeran are mentioned among those whose homes were consumed. Mr. Carroll resided "Towards Oliver's dock," while Capt. Killeran was located at "Milk Street and Battery-March."

John Kelley, of Providence, R. I., died in 1701–'02. His widow, Grace Kelley, refused administration of the estate, and in her stead the Town Council appointed Pardon Tillinghast, Jonathan Sprague and James Browne. (*Records of the Town of Providence.*)

In 1677, 61 families at Salem, Mass., representing 295 persons, who were in needy circumstances owing to King Philip's war, were given £44 5s from contributions collected in Ireland. This was a portion of "The Irish Charity." (Felt's *Annals of Salem.*)

Gen. Thomas Proctor was born in Ireland, 1739, and settled in Philadelphia, Pa. He entered the Patriot army in the Revolution, and rendered distinguished service at the battle of Brandywine and elsewhere. He was an artillery officer. He died in 1806.

Patrick Mark is mentioned in Charlestown, Mass., in 1685. He was then 55 years of age. His wife was named Sarah. Their children were Sarah, Peter, Hannah and Mercie. A daughter was killed by the Indians in 1691. (Wyman's *Genealogies and Estates.*)

Pittston, Me., was incorporated in 1779. Among the early settlers of the town were: Stephen Kenny, William Burke, Thomas Moore, Daniel Ring, Martin Hailey, Thomas Hailey, Joseph Hailey and William Hailey. (*Maine Historical and Genealogical Recorder.*)

James Given, a native of Ireland, born in 1777, participated in the Irish rebellion of 1798. Subsequently he came to this country and located at Fishkill, N. Y. A "useful and prominent citizen for 60 years." (*N. Y. Genealogical and Biographical Record*, Jan. 1893.)

James Boies, writing in 1749-'50, from Cork, Ireland, to Samuel Waldo of Boston, Mass., says: " My business here is to carry Passengers & Servants," meaning, of course, to America. He requests that letters be sent him "to ye care of m^r Winthrop, merch^t in Cork."

Lieut.-Col. Goffe, an Irishman, was, in 1760, ordered by Gen. Amherst to take a regiment of 800 men, raised in New Hampshire, and cut a road through the wilderness from "No. 4" to Crown Point, or more properly to the Green Mountains. (*History of Springfield, Vt.*)

Rev. Ezra Stiles, writing at Newport, R. I., Aug. 9, 1774, says: "Last month arrived at New Castle [Del.] the snow *Charlotte*, Capt. Gaffney, from Waterford, with 100 passengers, and the ship *Hope*, Capt. McClenachan, from Newry, with 200." (*Diary of Ezra Stiles.*)

Hon. Thomas Dongan, the Irish governor of the province of New York, 1683-'88, was a wise and just man. He founded representative government in New York, and the Charter of Liberties given the colonists at that time has greatly served to perpetuate his fame.

In a general return of Col. William Thomson's regiment of Rangers, Sept. 20, 1775, occur the names Lieutenant Richard Brown, a native of Ireland, and Lieut. David Monaghan. Of the drummers, three were born in Ireland. The command was operating in the South.

A paragraph in the *Virginia Historical Magazine* states that Davis Stockton came from Ireland, with Michael Woods, and lived for some time in Lancaster county, Pa. About 1734 Stockton went to Albermarle County, Va., where he patented large tracts of land. He died in 1760.

William Preston was born in Ireland, 1730. He was captain of a company of rangers in Virginia in 1755-'56, and was a member of the Virginia House of Burgesses in 1766, 1767, 1768 and 1769. During the Revolution he held important commands in southwest Virginia.

Sir William Johnson, an Irishman, "of Johnson Hall, in the County of Tryon, and Province of New York," in his will, 1774, mentions bequests to William Byrne, of Kingsborough; Patrick Daly ("now living with me"); and Mary McGrah, daughter of Christopher McGrah.

In June, 1794, Capt. Harding arrived at Portland, Me., from Ireland, in the brig *Eliza*. He brought about 200 passengers, men, women, and children, "chiefly farmers and weavers," an "honest and industrious set of people." (*Maine Historical and Genealogical Recorder.*)

Bryan Lefferty was attorney and private secretary to Sir William Johnson and became surrogate of Tryon county, N. Y. Johnson's will is believed to have been drawn up by him. Sir William's farm manager was an Irishman named Flood. (Simms' *Frontiersmen of New York.*)

In August, 1795, the brig *Eliza*, Capt. Wm. Fairfield, arrived at Salem, Mass., from Belfast, Ireland, with 89 emigrants. Among them were Samuel Breed, James and Sarah Dalrymple, John and William Lemon, the Dunlap family, and others of note. (Felt's *Annals of Salem.*)

One of the first military organizations in Albany, N. Y., enlisted in the Revolution, included David McCarthy, James McCarthy, John McEnry, David Sullivan, William Magie (Magee), Morris Welch, and other men whose names indicate Irish extraction. They signed the roll in June, 1775.

William McMahon was a taxpayer in Falmouth, Me., in 1777. Mention of him is made in the *Maine Genealogist and Recorder*. The same publication speaks of Edward Clarey and Patrick Manan as having belonged to Capt. John Hill's military company of Berwick, Me., in October, 1740.

The intentions of marriage between Benjamin Blanchard of Canterbury, N. H., and Bridget Fitzgerald of Contoocook, were posted up "at the Meeting House Door" in Rumford, N. H., March 26, 1739. (John C. Ordway in *Salem [Mass.] Press Historical and Genealogical Record, Vol. 2*.)

Thomas McLaughlin, of Bedford, N. H., was lieutenant in Capt. John Moore's company, Col. Stark's regiment, at the battle of Bunker Hill, June 17, 1775. McLaughlin was made captain of the company the morning after the battle, in place of Moore, promoted. (*Military Records of New Hampshire.*)

A Mrs. Hall and Mr. Keating arrived at New London, Conn., in August, 1770, from Dublin, in the brig *Patty*. Captain Forbes in the 58th year of his age died at Cork, Ireland, on March 5, 1791. He was a native of Hartford, Conn., and had resided in Ireland for many years prior to his death.

In 1790, Norwich, Conn., had a printer named Major John Byrne. About this time he went to Windham, Conn., where he published the *Phœnix* or *Windham Herald*. In 1795 he was the postmaster of Woodstock, Conn., and in 1807 a member of the Aqueduct Company of Windham.

The British evacuated Boston, Mass., March 17, 1776, and the Americans marched in and took possession. Washington, from his headquarters at Cambridge, authorized as the parole for the day: "Boston;" and the countersign: "St. Patrick." Gen. John Sullivan was brigadier of the day.

Keeney's Ferry, operated over the Connecticut River at Hartford, Conn., took its name from Richard Keeney, who was granted the privilege in Oct., 1712, by the Assembly. The ferry was discontinued by act of the Assembly in May, 1753. (*Rev. James H. O'Donnell, Norwalk, Conn.*)

Florence Maccarty bought land in Roxbury, Mass., in 1693. He was a provision dealer and contractor in Boston. He subsequently added to his Roxbury purchase, the property becoming known as the "Maccarty farm." The tract at one time comprised 60 acres. (Drake's *Town of Roxbury.*)

John O'Kane came to this country from Ireland in 1752. He was then 18 years of age. He located in or near Albany, N. Y., and married a daughter of Rev. Elisha Kent. On his marriage he is said to have dropped the "O" from his surname. (*N. Y. Genealogical and Biographical Record*, July, 1878.)

Michael Magee was a member of Capt. Marsh's Troop of Light Horse, of Essex, N. J., in the Revolution, and was wounded. Thomas Magee was a matross in Capt. Hugg's Western Company of Artillery, New Jersey. (*Official Register of the Officers and Men of New Jersey in the Revolutionary War.*)

William Henry came from Coleraine, Ireland, and established a manufactory of arms in Pennsylvania before the Revolution. In 1777 he was deputy commissary general and was active in sending supplies to the Patriot army at Valley Forge. He was elected to Congress in 1784, and died in 1786.

Matthew, John and Thomas Kilpatrick (also written Gillpatrick) came from Ireland in the early part of the 18th century and settled in Warren and Ware, Mass. In time the name was condensed to Patrick. John Patrick, of the family, was commissioned a lieutenant in the Patriot forces, Feb. 5, 1776.

Among the sufferers in the French and Indian war, sometimes called Gov. Shirley's war (1744-'49), was Michael Dogan, an Irishman. "He listed at Philadelphia, a soldier for Louisbourg, and was taken in his passage by a French" warship. He sickened, recovered, but had a fatal relapse. (*Drake.*)

James Devereaux was born at Wexford, Ireland, in 1766. He came to Salem, Mass., in 1780, with his uncle, John Murphy. In 1792 Devereaux married Sally Crowninshield of Salem. Later, he commanded the ship *Franklin*, said to have been the first merchant vessel from the United States to visit Japan

Capt. James Neall of New Hampshire had a group of scouts, in 1755, and was engaged in guarding the frontiers of said province. The scouts included Sergt. Philip Johnson, Francis Orr, James Rowe, William Mack and John McMahon. (*Military History of New Hampshire, Adjutant-General's Report, 1866*.

Here are two inscriptions from the Granary Burial Ground, Boston, Mass.: (1) "Here lyes y* body of Sarah Mahoney, Dau'r of Mr. Cain Mahoney, of Marblehead, aged 26 years, Died Nov. 29, 1734." (2) "Here lies the Body of Mrs. Elizabeth Kelly, wife of Mr. Patrick Kelly, aged 28 years, Died Sept. 25, 1758."

Andrew Brown was a native of Ireland, born about 1744. He was educated at Trinity College, Dublin, came to this country and fought in the patriot ranks at the battle of Bunker Hill. In 1777 he was made Muster-Master-General in the Patriot army. He died at Philadelphia, Pa., in 1793. (Drake's *American Biography*.)

Hugh Williamson was a member of the North Carolina House of Commons in 1782 and 1785; he was also elected to the Continental Congress. He was a native of Pennsylvania. His father, an Irishman, had been a clothier in Dublin, and came to this country in 1730. (Wheeler's *Historical Sketches of North Carolina*.)

George Conn emigrated from Ireland about 1720 and eventually settled in Harvard, Mass. His son, John, was born at Harvard, 1740, and located in Ashburnham, Mass., probably about 1761. John was lieutenant in a company of Minute Men and was with his command at Cambridge, Mass., 1775. He died in 1803.

Patrick Burn, of Wenham, Mass., participated in the Cape Breton expedition (Louisburg), 1744-'49. Later, he and others petitioned for an allowance on account of services and sufferings. The committee of war was ordered to pay the selectmen of Wenham £7 "for the use of said Burn." (Drake's *French and Indian War*.)

From the Town Records of Boston, Mass., Nov. 8, 1737: "Capt. James Finney Messrs. John Karr and William Hall Executed a Bond of the Penalty of Six Hundred Pounds to Indemnify the Town on Acco^t. of One Hundred and Sixty two Passengers Imported by the said Finney in the Snow Charming Molly from Ireland* * *"

At a meeting in 1744 of the proprietors of the common and undivided lands belonging to the town of Kittery, Me., among those drawing tracts of land were: John Gowen, Nicholas Gowen, Andrew

Haley, John More, Joseph Mitchell, James Troy, Andrew Neal, and Samuel Ford. (*Maine Historical and Genealogical Recorder.*)

Thomas Butler settled in Kittery, Me., before 1695. He is grandiloquently described by a modern writer as "of the ancient English house of Ormonde." Perhaps it would have been nearer the point to say that Butler was an Irishman "of the house of Ormonde." He had a son, Thomas, born at Berwick, Me., 1698.

From the Town Records of Boston, Mass., Nov. 8, 1737: "Hugh Ramsey, John Weire, and William Moore, Executed a Bond of the Penalty of one Thousand Pounds to Indemnify the Town from Charge on acc°. of Three Hundred and Eighty One Passengers Imported by Capt. Daniel Gibbs in the Ship Sagamore from Ireland.* * *"

"Daniel ye Son of Darby and Elizabeth Mallonee" was baptized, in Barbadoes, 1679. The same year mention is made of Teag Conner, of the parish of St. Michael, Barbadoes. "Mary ye Wife of Morgan Murphy" of the parish of St. James, Barbadoes, was buried in 1679, as was also "Cornelius ye Son of Dearman Driskell." (Hotten's *Lists.*)

John Kehoo and Edward Dalton, two young Irishmen, came to Salem, Mass., in 1776. "They were both remarkably handsome, and promising men, and by their circumspect conduct and industrious habits, soon gained the respect and confidence of the community." Kehoo was lost at sea while aboard the privateer *Centipede*, in 1781.

In Felt's *Annals of Salem, Mass.*, it is stated under date of April 20, 1681, "a ketch, Capt. Edward Henfield, picked up a boat with Capt. Andrew and six of his crew, 150 leagues from Cape Cod. These persons, so rescued, belonged to a Dublin ship bound to Virginia. She sank on the 18th, with sixteen men and three women, who perished."

Daniel Gookin " of Cargoline, near Cork, Ireland," commenced a plantation in Virginia in 1621-'22. He is said to have been born in England and to have "settled in Ireland." He came to Virginia with fifty men of his own and thirty passengers, and located at a place called Mary's Mount, near Newport News. (*Virginia Historical Magazine.*)

At a town meeting in Boston, March 12, 1771, "A letter from that celebrated Patriot, Dr Lucas of Ireland, owning the Receipt of one transmitted him by a Committee of this Town together with the Pamphlet relative to the horred Massacre in Boston, March, 5, 1770 —was read and attended to with the highest satisfaction." (*Boston Town Records.*)

From the Town Records of Boston, Mass., Sept. 19, 1744: "At the Desire of His Excellency the Governour The Select men Sent up to the Almshouse Sixteen Girls & Three Boys & a Woman arrived here yesterday from Cape Breton who were taken About Six Weeks since by a French Privateer [they] being bound from Ireland to Philadelphia***"

From the *Connecticut Gazette*, Jan. 5, 1764: "Just imported from Dublin, in the brig *Darby*, a parcel of Irish servants, both men and women, to be sold cheap, by Israel Boardman, at Stamford." The people thus advertised were doubtless of the "Redemptioner" class, to be disposed of for a term of years, to pay for the expense of bringing them over.

From the Boston Selectmen's Records, Jan. 15, 1715: "Jarvice Bethell, sho maker Late of Ireland who wth his wife came by the way of New found Land into this Town in August Last is admitted an Inhabit^t on condition, he finde suretyes to ye Satisfaction of ye Sel. men to ye value of 100 [£], Since its consented y^t Mr. Shannons bond Shall Suffice."

Hon. John Fanchereau Grimke was a colonel in the Revolutionary army and judge of the Supreme Court of South Carolina. Early in life he wedded Mary Smith. She was of Irish and English stock, and was the great granddaughter of the second landgrave of South Carolina, and descended on her mother's side from the famous Irish chieftain, Roger Moore.

Daniel McCurtin, believed to be of Maryland, was in the Patriot army at the siege of Boston. He kept a journal of his observations and experiences. The same has been published and narrates many interesting incidents of the siege. The journal may be found in *Papers Relating Chiefly to the Maryland Line During the Revolution*, edited by Thomas Balch.

The town of Sterling, Conn., was named in honor of Dr. Henry Sterling, an Irish physician and surgeon, who was located in Providence, R. I., before and during the Revolution. When the patriots from Providence destroyed the British armed vessel *Gaspee*, June 10, 1772, Dr. Sterling responded to a summons to attend the wounded commander of the *Gaspee*.

Timothy Murphy, an Irish physician, came to this country in 1776 and settled in Monmouth county, New Jersey. He engaged in farming; married Mary Garrison, granddaughter of Richard Hartshorne, of that county, who was a member of the Colonial Council and of the Assembly of the Province. Murphy served in the Patriot army during the Revolution.

Nehemiah Walter was sent by his father from Ireland to America, about 1674, to serve an apprenticeship to an upholsterer in Boston. Having a fondness for books he, with the consent of his father, attended college and graduated in 1680. He settled in Roxbury, Mass., and married Sarah, a daughter of Increase Mather. (*N. E. Hist., Gen. Register*, Jan., 1853.)

Rev. James Hillhouse was born in Ireland, and in 1720 came to America. He settled in Connecticut and married a great granddaughter of Capt. John Mason. Their son, William Hillhouse, became a member of the Continental Congress and was a cavalry officer in the Revolution. He represented his town in 106 semi-annual sessions of the legislature.

Sometime in 1745 as James McQuade and Robert Burns of Bedford, N. H., were returning from Penacook to their homes, whither they went to procure corn for their families, they were fired on by Indians who appeared to be lying in wait for the opportunity. McQuade was shot down and killed, but his companion escaped. (Drake's *French and Indian War*.)

The Rev. Robert Morris, who was pastor of the First Church in Greenwich, Conn., in 1785, was "born and brought up in N. York. His parents came from Ireland, the Father a rigid Churchman, his mother a Roman Catholic. He living and being brot up with a Baptist at N. York became one." (*Rev. Ezra Stiles, quoted by Rev. James H. O'Donnell, Norwalk, Conn.*)

We find Joseph Manly in Conventry, Conn., in 1786; Patrick Butler in Hartford, and Richard Kearney in New London in 1793. In the list of expenses paid by Connecticut for the capture of Ticonderoga and adjacent posts, occurs the name of an Irishman: "To Patrick Thomas, for boarding prisoners, £1, 5s." (Rev. J. H. O'Donnell in *Catholic Transcript*, Hartford, Conn.)

On July 2, 1788, Captain Chapman, and nine emigrants from Ireland, were drowned a short distance from the shore of Fisher's Island. He had just arrived with about 20 emigrants, some of whom were ill. In attempting to land the latter at a spot where they were to be placed in quarantine, all perished. (Rev. J. H. O'Donnell in *Catholic Transcript*, Hartford, Conn.)

John J. Henry's parents came from Coleraine, Ireland. John was born in Lancaster, Pa., 1758, and was with Arnold's expedition to Quebec. He was captured by the British and kept a prisoner for nine months. On being released, he was offered a lieutenancy in the Pennsylvania line, but desired a captaincy in the Virginia line. Ill health interfered somewhat with his military career.

According to Hotten's *Lists*, Brian Kelley, aged 20, embarked for Virginia in the vessel *Safety*, 1635. Among those to be transported to "y⁰ Barbadoes," 1635, were Dennis MacBrian, Teague Nacton, Dermond O'Bryan and Margaret Conway. They embarked in the *Alexander*. Mary Driskell, of St. James' parish, Barbadoes, was buried 1678. Dorothy Callahan, of Barbadoes, was buried Aug. 10, 1679.

Miss Virginia Baker of Warren, R. I., author of a "History of Warren in the War of the Revolution," writes us : "Perhaps you will be interested to know that the first Irishman known to have settled in Warren was one John O'Kelley. I think he arrived in town prior to 1770. . . . I have located real estate that he owned." Miss Baker also informs us that some of his descendants are still to be found in Warren.

Cornelius Merry, an Irishman, of Northampton, Mass., had a grant of land in 1663. He married Rachel Ballard. Their children were John, who "died soon;" John (2d), born in 1665; Sarah, born 1668; Rachel, 1670; Cornelius, Leah, and perhaps others. Cornelius, the father, participated in the "Falls fight" against the Indians. After the war he removed to Long Island, N. Y. (Savage's *Genealogical Dictionary*.)

John Lamb, who was captain of a brig called the *Irish Gimlte* is found at New London, Conn., in 1774; Lawrence Sullivan "of Connecticut" was taken prisoner by the British at the battle of

Bunker Hill, and was released February 24, 1776; Captain Richard McCarthy of New London, was wrecked in a storm off Plum Island, May 27, 1779, when he and five sailors perished. (*Rev. James H. O'Donnell, Norwalk, Conn.*)

Capt. Philip Mortimer, who came from Ireland, was one of the selectmen of Middletown, Conn., in 1749. He was a rope maker, was very wealthy, and donoted Mortimer cemetery to the town. Being childless, he sent to Ireland for his niece to come out and become his adopted daughter. The son of Capt. John Reid, Mortimer's partner, was despatched to Boston with a coach and four and escorted her to Middletown.

Glancing through Deane's "History of Scituate, Mass.," the other day, we found mention of Richard Fitzgerald, "a veteran Latin schoolmaster." He wedded Margaret Snowdon, of Scituate, in 1729. Doubtless he was one of the many Irish teachers who abounded in the American colonies at that and subsequent periods. The American-Irish Historical Society has already published the names, and something concerning the career, of about forty such.

Charles Clinton was a native of County Longford, Ireland, and was born in 1690. He and his friends, numbering about 200, chartered a vessel and sailed from Dublin in 1729 for Philadelphia, Pa. After a passage lasting 139 days the captain, inadvertently or by design, landed them on Cape Cod, Mass. Ninety-six of the ship's company had died on the voyage. One of Clinton's sons, George, became governor of New York.

An Irish colony, consisting of sixteen families, was settled about 1740, under the patronage of Sir William Johnson, himself an Irishman, on a tract a few miles southwest of Fort Hamilton, N. Y., in the town of Glen. The settlers erected dwellings, cleared land and planted orchards. Indian hostilities, however, prevented the success of the settlement, and the pioneers returned to Ireland. (J. R. Simms' *Frontiersmen of New York.*)

Robert Dunlap was a native of the County Antrim, Ireland, and was born in 1715. He embarked for America in the spring of 1736. The vessel, with nearly 200 emigrants aboard, was wrecked at the Isle of Sable and nearly one half of the passengers perished. The survivors, including Dunlap, managed to reach Canso and were then taken to Cape Ann, Mass. Governor Dunlap of Maine (elected in 1833), was a descendant of Robert, the Irishman.

The records of Trinity Church, New York city, contain mention of the following marriages: Hugh Kelly and Elizabeth Griffin, 1746; Ralph Steel and Mary Branegan, 1747; John Trotter and Ann Hogan, 1748; John Cusick and Mary Freeman, 1748; John Hurley and Elizabeth Hannon, 1748; Patrick Hawley and Jane Ament, 1748; Jeremiah Dailey and Margaret Fitzgerald, 1748; Patrick Boyd and Mary Peltreau, 1748; Patrick Martin and Rozannah O'Neil, 1748.

The Boston *News Letter*, Sept. 12, 1720, has an advertisement in which it is stated that an Irish man servant, Edward Coffee, had run away from his master, Stephen Winchester of Brookline, Mass. Coffee was probably a bond servant or redemptioner. He is described as about twenty years of age, with "cinnamon coloured breeches with six puffs tied at the knees with ferret ribbon." He also had "a wig tied with a black ribbon." A reward was offered for his capture.

Capt. James Magee, "a convivial, noble-hearted Irishman," commanded an American privateer in the Revolution. In the winter of 1779 his ship was driven ashore near Plymouth, Mass., during a terrible storm, and 79 of the crew were frozen to death. Twenty-eight of the survivors were rescued by the men of Plymouth. Drake's *Town of Roxbury, Mass.*, states that in 1798 Capt. Magee bought an estate in Roxbury. In 1819 William Eustis purchased the estate of Magee's widow.

The Society of the Friendly Sons of St. Patrick, Philadelphia, Pa., was instituted on March 17, 1771. No creed lines were drawn, and in the organization "Catholics, Presbyterians, Quakers, and Episcopalians were united like a band of brothers." Stephen Moylan, brother of the Catholic bishop of Cork, Ireland, was the first president. The Society of the Friendly Sons of St. Patrick, New York city, was founded in 1784. Daniel McCormick, a Presbyterian, was the first president.

In 1644, Roger Williams, arriving at Boston, from England, brought with him letters from members of the British parliament to "leading men of the Bay" in which, counseling friendship, mention is made of undesirable "neighbours you are likely to find near unto you in Virginia, and the unfriendly visits from the west of England and from Ireland." It so happened that, eventually, Roger Williams himself became "undesirable" and "unfriendly" to the self-sufficient rulers of "the Bay."

Thomas Healey is mentioned as of Cambridge, Mass., in 1635, and William Healey in 1645. John Joyce was an early resident of Lynn, Mass., and removed to Sandwich, Mass., about 1637. David Kelly was of Boston as early as 1664, and belonged to the artillery company there. Stephen Hart was of Cambridge, Mass., in 1632; Edmund Hart of Weymouth, Mass., 1634; John Hart of Salem, Mass., 1638; Thomas Hart of Ipswich, Mass., 1648. (Farmer's *Genealogical Register*.)

In a Virginia regiment, of which George Washington was colonel, long before the Revolution, appear the following surnames: Barrett, Bryan, Burns, Burke, Carroll, Coleman, Conner, Connerly, Conway, Coyle, Daily, Deveeny, Devoy, Donahough, Ford, Gorman, Hennesy, Kennedy, Lowry, McBride, McCoy, McGrath, McGuire, McKan, McLaughlin, Martin, Moran, Murphy, Powers, etc. The regiment participated in the struggles against the French and Indians. (*Virginia Historical Magazine*.)

Dennis Rochford, of County Wexford, Ireland, and his wife Mary, came to Pennsylvania with William Penn in 1682, on the ship *Welcome*. All or nearly all the passengers were Quakers. Two daughters of Dennis and Mary died on the voyage. The passengers were described as "people of consequence" and as "people of property." Dennis was a member of the Assembly in 1683. (Scharf-Wescott *History of Philadelphia, Pa.*, quoted in Vol. VI, Transactions of the Kansas State Historical Society.)

In the "Great Swamp fight" in Southern Rhode Island, during King Philip's war, 1675-'76, were the following soldiers from Connecticut, among others: James Murphy, Daniel Tracy, Edward Larkin, James Welch and John Roach. The town of Norwalk, Conn., subsequently gave Roach, as a gratuity, a tract of land "consisting of twelve acres more or less, layed out upon the west side of the West Rock, so called." In the Norwalk records Roach is spoken of as a soldier in the "Direful Swamp Fight."

Eaton's Annals of Warren, Me., mention two Irish schoolmasters there. They were John O'Brien and John Sullivan. O'Brien was "a native of Craig, near Cork," and taught in Warren for many years, beginning at about the close of the Revolution. He was "an elegant penman and a good accountant." He married a daughter of Col. Starrett. Sullivan was a native of Dublin, Ireland, and began teaching in Warren about 1792. He was of "never failing good humor." He died in Boston, Mass.

Martin I. J. Griffin of Philadelphia, Pa., mentions Thomas Burke, the one-eyed member of the Continental Congress and governor of North Carolina, of whom Wheeler's *Historical Sketches of North Carolina* says: "No public functionary was ever employed by the state in more troubled times, none more active or talented, none suffered more, none less known to posterity. He was a native of Ireland and of the most finished education." It was said of him that he publicly professed and openly avowed the Catholic faith.

Here is an example of how certain names sometimes undergo a change: A legislative act was passed in 1806 providing that "John O'Neil, Jun., of Madison, in the county of Kennebec [Maine], shall be allowed to take the name of John Neil; James O'Neil, of said Madison, shall be allowed to take the name of James Neil; Samuel O'Neil, of Norridgewalk, shall be allowed to take the name of Samuel Neil." (From *List of Persons whose Names Have Been Changed*, etc., published by the state of Massachusetts, Boston, 1893.)

George Berkeley, "the Kilkenny scholar," Dean of Derry and later Bishop of Cloyne, visited Boston in 1731. His visit is thus mentioned in John Walker's manuscript diary (in possession of the Massachusetts Historical Society): "Sept. 12, 1731; in ye morn Dean George Barkley preacht in ye Chapell from ye 1st Epistle to Timothy, ye 3^d Chap., Verse 16, and a fine Sermon, according to my opinion I never heard such an one. A very great auditory." By the "Chapell" was meant the King's Chapel, still in use in Boston.

From an entry in the *New England Historic, Genealogical Register*, Jan., 1893, we learn that Capt. John McCarty of New London, Conn., died while on a return voyage from the West Indies in 1804. His wife died soon after, leaving four young children, including Elizabeth, who married Samuel Forman, of Syracuse, N. Y.; Rebecca, who married Schuyler Van Rensselaer of Albany, N. Y., and Abby, who married Sanders Van Rensselaer, brother to Schuyler. Capt. Richard McCarty, believed to be father or brother of Capt. John, was lost at sea in 1779.

At a meeting of the selectmen of Boston, Mass., April 15, 1737, a communication was mentioned as having been received from Capt. Samuel Waterhouse. The latter stated that he was "twelve weeks from London and seven from Cork; that smallpox had broken out on the voyage, afflicting four of his ship's company. One of these was put ashore, one died at sea, and two recovered. The ship having been cleansed, the Boston selectmen gave him permission to "come up from Nantasket to Spectacle Island" and drop anchor near the hospital there. (*Report of the Boston Record Commission.*)

Hon. James Buchanan, president of the United States, has left this statement concerning himself: "My father, James Buchanan, was a native of the County Donegal, in the Kingdom of Ireland. His family was respectable but their pecuniary circumstances were limited. He emigrated to the United States before the date of the Definitive Treaty of Peace with Great Britain; having sailed from ———— [no port stated] in the brig *Providence*, bound for Philadelphia, in 1783. He was then in the 22d year of his age." Quoted in George Ticknor Curtis' *Life of James Buchanan*, President.)

In a volume published by the state of New York (Albany, 1860), record is found of marriage licenses, issued by the secretary of the province, previous to 1784. Among the names mentioned are: Edward Briscow and Jane McDermont, 1736; Matthew Sweeny and Mary Thorn, 1756; Patrick Hyne and Hannah Van Sice, 1757; Andries Van Schaick and Alida Hogan, 1757; Owen Sullivan and Hannah Orstin, 1759; Wynant Van Zant and Jane Colgan, 1760; Rynear Van Yeveron and Hannah Hogan, 1772; John Moore and Mary Van Dyck, 1772; Martin Van Haugh and Judith Carroll, 1775.

In the Minutes of the Boston Selectmen, 1727, we find mention of the following "Strangers warned to Depart Accord[n] to Law": John White, an Irishman from Dedham; Robert Phenne, an Irishman from Wells; William Nugel, an Irishman from Philadelphia; Robert Sterling, an Irishman from Rutland; Patrick Jorden from Virginia; James Dawley, an Irishman from Lisborn; Joseph Doyle from Rhode Island. These men were doubtless worthy enough, but, perhaps, could find no one to "go their bond," and thus secure the town against the possibility of their becoming, at some time, a public charge.

For the "expedition against Crown Point," 1756, New Hampshire raised a regiment of 700 men, commanded by Col. Nathaniel Meserve of Portsmouth. In this regiment were included the following: Daniel Murphy, James Meloney, Darby Sullivan, John McMahone, Daniel Kelley, James O'Neil, Jer. Connor, Daniel Carty, Benjamin Mooney, Michael Johnson, Darbey Kelley, John Meloney, James Molloy, James Kelly, John Welch, Thomas Carty, William Kelley, Bryan Tweny (Sweeny?), James McLaughlin, John McLaughlin, Thomas McLaughlin, and others bearing typical Irish names. (*Military History of New Hampshire, Adjutant-General's Report*, Concord, 1866.)

From the Boston Selectmen's Records, Aug. 9, 1736: " By a List from the Impost office, It appearing that Nineteen Transports were just Imported from Cork in Ireland, in the Brig' Bootle, Robert Boyd Commander, accordingly the said Master was sent for, Who appear'd And the Select men Ordered him to take effectual Care to prevent any of the said Transports from coming on Shoar from said Vessell, the said Master promised Accordingly that they should not come on Shoar, That he was obliged by his orders to Carry them to Virginia, Whither he was bound, and that in the meantime he would keep a Strict Watch on board his said Vessell to prevent their escape."

James Cochran, an Irish boy, is mentioned in the Massachusetts records. He was captured by Indians, but escaped and brought back a couple of scalps as evidence of his experience. The *Boston News Letter*, April 29, 1725, says of him: "James Cochran, ye youth that came into Brunswick with two scalps, came to town on Monday last, and on Tuesday produced ye same scalps before ye Honorable Lieutenant Governor and Council, for which he received a reward of two hundred pounds. And for ye further encouragement of young men and others to perform bold and hardy actions in ye Indian war, His Honor ye Lieutenant Governor has been pleased to make him sargeant in ye forces."

A gallant officer, who has almost been forgotten, was Gen. John Greaton of the Revolution. He was a native of Ireland. Augustus Parker, writing in the Boston *Transcript*, says of him that he belonged to the first company of Minute Men raised in America, in 1775, and was chosen major, lieutenant-colonel, and colonel of Heath's regiment. After the battle of Lexington he was engaged in the skirmishes about Boston, until he joined that memorable expedition to Quebec in the winter through the woods of Maine, where the army suffered untold hardships. He served through the war, was one of Washington's most trusted officers, was mustered out October, 1783, and died the following December, worn out in the service of his country. Gen. Greaton's father kept the Greyhound tavern on Washington street, opposite Vernon street, in Roxbury, Mass.

Rev. Cotton Mather was born in Boston, Mass., Feb. 12, 1663. He was a Puritan, hard and fast. In 1700 he delivered a sermon in honor of the arrival of Gov. Bellomont, calling it a "Pillar of Gratitude." In this sermon occurs the following: "There has been formidable Attempts of Satan and his Son to Unsettle us: But what an overwhelming blast from Heaven has defeated all those attempts. . . . . At length it was proposed that a Colony of Irish might be sent over to check the growth of this Countrey: An Happy Revolution spoil'd that Plot: and many an one of more general consequence Than That!" Mather was rather late in his opposition to Irish comers, for they had been arriving in this "Countrey" before he was born. Were he alive to-day he would doubtless realize that instead of checking the country's growth, they have greatly contributed to that growth.

Passing through Bridgeport, Conn., by train recently, we recalled the Rev. Robert Ross of that place. He was a son of Irish parents, and was ordained to the Congregational ministry in 1753. His biographer states that he was a remarkable man, six feet in height and well proportioned. His presence was imposing, and his ruffled shirt, wig and cocked hat seemed peculiarly in keeping with it. But he most strongly impressed himself upon the community through the warmth of his patriotism, and the decisiveness of his political convictions. He became a man of influence on the patriotic side and proportionally obnoxious to the royalists. At the outbreak of the Revolutionary War he preached on the text, "For the divisions of Reuben there were great searchings of heart." A company of soldiers, raised to join the invasion of Canada in the fall of 1775, mustered in his door-yard and was commended to God in a fervent prayer by him before starting on their expedition.

The dangers encountered by Irish immigrants who came over in the old days of sailing vessels is well illustrated by the following incident: The ship *Lime* with 123 passengers sailed from Portrush,

Ireland, July 26, 1738, bound for Boston. Three days after leaving Portrush she was leaking badly, so she put into Killybegs where twelve days were spent making repairs. She again sailed, but had to put into Galway to be again repaired. While at Galway, John Cate, the master, died of smallpox, and Matthias Haines, the only mate, was afflicted with the same disease. While at Killybegs and Galway 25 of the passengers deserted the ship, and but little blame could attach to them for so doing. With the captain dead and the mate sick, the contractors hired Gabriel Black as master of the vessel. She finally sailed from Galway on Sept. 19, and reached Boston harbor Nov. 16, 1738. Mention of the incident may be found in the *N. E. Historic, Genealogical Register*, Oct., 1897.

In 1630, Governor John Winthrop and others of the Massachusetts Bay Colony "hired and dispatched away Mr. William Pearse, with his ship of about two hundred tons, for Ireland to buy more" provisions. As he did not return as soon as expected, "many were the fears of people that Mr. Pearce who was sent to Ireland to fetch provisions, was cast away or taken by pirates." In February, 1631, however, he arrived at Boston, Mass., bringing the following supplies: 34 hogsheads of wheat meal, 15 hogsheads of peas, 4 hogsheads of oatmeal, 4 hogsheads of beef and pork, 15 cwt. of cheese, buttersuet, etc. These supplies were in good condition, and a day of thanksgiving was ordered by the governor." (Frothingham's *Charlestown* and Drake's *Boston*.) A second ship appears to have arrived about this time, for the colonists near by "lifted up their eyes and saw two ships coming in, and presently the newes came to their eares, says one among them, that they were come from Ireland full of victualls."

In Stackpole's *History of Durham, Me.*, is an interesting reference to Martin Rourk, at one time town clerk of that place. Rourk was born in Ireland about 1760, and came to America about 1773. He spent two years in his uncle's store at St. John's, and went to Boston, Mass., in 1775. He became clerk in the company of Capt. Lawrence of the Patriot army, and subsequently married his widow. In May, 1775, Martin Rourk is mentioned as in a picket guard, having enlisted in April of that year. He reënlisted several times, was at Ticonderoga in 1776, and is mentioned as a sergeant after 1777. He settled in Durham, Me., about 1784, and in 1796 bought a twenty-acre lot of Thomas Mitchell, was town clerk in 1790–1807, and is spoken of as an excellent penman. He was also "the foremost school teacher" of Durham. He died in 1807. His children were Jane, John, Hannah, William, David, Samuel, Silence, Cyrus, and Jacob H. Some of these had the name changed to Roak before 1820. John, one of the sons, wedded Joanna Larrabee and had seven children.

Printed by Libri Plureos GmbH in Hamburg, Germany